ANIMAL
MOVEMENT

First edition for the United States, Canada,
and the Philippines published 1991
by Barron's Educational Series, Inc.

© Copyright by Aladdin Books, Ltd 1991

Design David West Children's Book Design
Illustrations Kate Taylor
Text Anita Ganeri
Picture research Angela Graham

Created and designed by
N.W. Books
28 Percy Street
London W1P 9FF

All inquiries should be addressed to:
Barron's Educational Series, Inc.
250 Wireless Boulevard
Hauppauge, NY 11788

International Standard Book No. 0-8120-6238-8

Library of Congress Catalog Card No. 91-9964

Library of Congress Cataloging-in Publication Data

Ganeri, Anita, 1961-
Movement / by Anita Ganeri : illustrated by Kate Taylor.
p.   cm. -- (Animal questions and answers)
Summary: Questions and answers explore how different
animals move in different ways and at different speeds.
ISBN 0-8120-6238-8
1. Animal locomotion--Juvenile literature. [1. Animal
locomotion--Miscellanea. 2. Questions and answers.]
I. Taylor, Kate, ill. II. Title. II. Series.
QP301.G36   1991
591.1'852--dc20   91-9964   CIP   AC

Printed in Belgium
1234   987654321

QUESTIONS AND ANSWERS ABOUT
ANIMAL MOVEMENT

Barron's
New York • Toronto

How do animals move?

Animals move in lots of different ways. They walk, run and hop. They swing, swim, fly and glide. Some can walk on water. Some even walk upside down! And a few just hitch rides on other animals. This book tells you which animals move fast, which move slowly and which animals let others do the hard work for them!

Which animals move very slowly?

Even when they are hungry, turtles, sloths, slugs and snails move very slowly indeed. It would take a slug about 15 minutes to crawl across these two pages. A snail could do it in under three minutes!

Which animal can run the fastest?

Cheetahs can sprint at over 60 miles an hour. This is twice as fast as the fastest human sprinter. Cheetahs have very bendy backbones to help them run faster. They quickly get tired, though. After about 500 yards, they have to rest and get their breath back.

Which animals jump, but don't run?

Because of their strange shape, kangaroos would find it very difficult to run. They would probably fall over their long feet! So they jump instead, using their big, strong back legs. They can leap over eight yards in one bound.

Which animals can jump the highest?

For their size, fleas can jump higher than any other creatures. They can jump about 150 times their own height. This would be like you jumping over a pile of 30 houses, one on top of the other!

Which birds can fly backwards?

Hummingbirds can fly backwards, forwards, sideways, up, down and even upside down. They also hover quietly in front of flowers so they can eat the sweet nectar deep inside. To do this, the birds beat their wings up to 90 times a second. This makes the humming noise which gives them their name.

Can all birds fly?

All birds have wings, but not all of them can fly. Ostriches can't fly but they are very fast runners. On their long legs they can run faster than a horse. Kiwis can't fly and neither can penguins.

13

What has wings for flying, but no feathers?

Birds are not the only animals that can fly. Insects and bats don't have feathers, but they do have wings for flying. Bats fly around at night, looking for food. Their wings are made of leathery skin stretched across their very long fingers.

Which animals can fly without wings?
Some frogs, lizards and squirrels can glide. The flying frog spreads its feet and flattens its body to glide. Others use flaps of skin between their front and back legs.

Can monkeys fly?

Monkeys can't really fly, but they swing through the trees so fast they look as if they are flying. Monkeys have arms that are twice as long as their bodies. They use them to swing at high speed from branch to branch.

How can fish fly?

Flying fish shoot out of the water to escape from hungry enemies. Then they glide above the water, using their fins as wings. To get extra lift, they bounce off the surface of the water every 40 yards or so.

Which fish would sink if it stopped swimming?

Most fish have a special air-filled pouch inside their bodies, called a swim bladder. It keeps the fish afloat in the water, even when they stop swimming. Sharks do not have swim bladders, though. If they stopped swimming, they would sink!

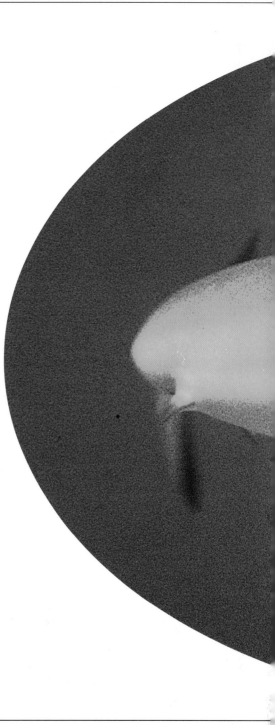

How do fish swim?
Fish use their fins to help them swim. They beat their tail fins to push their bodies through the water. They use their other fins to keep themselves upright and to change direction.

Which animals take passengers?
Buffalo, rhinos and giraffes carry birds around with them which eat their ticks. These "tickbirds" don't have to travel this way. They can hop and fly too.

Which animal hitches a ride?

Sea anemones hitch rides on hermit crabs. A crab may have up to ten anemones covering its shell. The anemones eat scraps of the crab's food. In return, they protect the crab by stinging its enemies with their poisoned tentacles.

Which creatures can walk on water?

Pond skaters can walk across water without falling in. Water is covered with a very thin, stretchy skin. The pond skater has thick pads of waxy hair on its feet so that it can skate across the skin without breaking it.

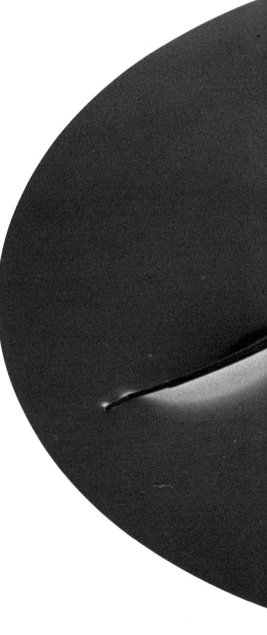

Can all animals swim?
Giraffes are such an odd shape that they probably can't swim, even in an emergency. There is a story of a giraffe that fell into some water by accident. It sank without even trying to swim.

How do snakes slither?

Most snakes slither by pushing their bodies along the ground in a curving movement. As their scales rub over stones and soil, though, they wear out. Snakes shed their old skins and grow new ones up to four times a year.

Do worms slither?

Worms' bodies are divided into lots of segments. They move by pushing and pulling these segments along. Worms also have hairy bristles on their bodies. These help them grip as they dig through soil.

Which animals swing by their tails?

Spider monkeys have very long, very strong tails. The monkeys swing through the jungle trees looking for food. They can hang from a branch by their tails alone, leaving both hands free for eating!

Which animals use their tails to steer in midair?

Gerbils can hop very fast on their long back legs to escape from enemies. They can also jump high into the air and out of reach. They use their long tails for balance as they hop, and to change direction when they are in midair.

Which animals can walk upside down?

Geckos can walk up walls and windows and even hang upside down on ceilings. They have tiny hooks under their flat toes. These catch on to even the smallest bumps on a surface so the gecko does not fall off.

Which animals have suction pads on their feet?

Mountain goats can leap from one rocky ledge to another without slipping. Their hooves are specially notched to give a strong, suction-like grip.

Index

Photographs
Cover and pages 8, 26/27: Planet Earth; pages 4, 12/13, 15, 17, 29: Bruce Coleman; pages 6, 19 23: Frank Lane Picture Agency; page 10: Ardea; pages 20, 24: Oxford Scientific Films.